*Initiation
and the
Great Mysteries*

By C. H. Vail

Copyright © 2021 Lamp of Trismegistus. All rights reserved. No part of this publication may be reproduced or transmitted in any form or by any means, electronic or mechanical, including photocopying, recording, or by any information storage and retrieval system, without permission in writing from Lamp of Trismegistus. Reviewers may quote brief passages.

ISBN: 978-1-63118-537-3

Esoteric Classics

Other Books in this Series and Related Titles

Masonic and Rosicrucian History by M P Hall & H Voorhis (978-1-63118-486-4)

The Kabbalah of Masonry & Related Writings by E Levi &c (978-1-63118-453-6)

Some Deeper Aspects of Masonic Symbolism by A E Waite (978-1-63118-461-1)

Masonic Symbolism of King Solomon's Temple by A Mackey &c (978-1-63118-442-0)

The Old Past Master by Carl H Claudy (978-1-63118-464-2)

The Influence of Pythagoras on Freemasonry and Other Essays (978-1-63118-404-8)

The Symbols and Legends of Masonry by C H Vail (978-1-63118-504-5)

Rosicrucians and Speculative Masonry in the Seventeenth Century (978-1-63118-489-5)

The Two Great Pillars of Boaz and Jachin by A Mackey &c (978-1-63118-433-8)

The Regius Poem or Halliwell Manuscript by King Solomon (978-1-63118-447-5)

The Lost Keys of Freemasonry or The Secret of Hiram Abiff (978-1-63118-427-7)

The Master Mason's Handbook by J S M Ward (978-1-63118-474-1)

Masonic Symbolism of the Apron & the Altar by various (978-1-63118-428-4)

Symbolism and Discourses on the Entered Apprentice, Fellowcraft and Master Mason Blue Lodge Degrees by various (978-1-63118-413-0)

Freemasonry & Catholicism by Max Heindel (978-1-63118-508-3)

American Indian Freemasonry by A C Parker (978-1-63118-460-4)

Freemasonry, Mithraism and the Ancient Mysteries by various (978-1-63118-407-9)

The Ceremony of Initiation: Analysis & Commentary (978-1-63118-473-4)

Masonic Life of George Washington by Albert G Mackey (978-1-63118-457-4)

The Janeites, The Man Who Would Be King and Other Stories of Freemasonry by Rudyard Kipling (978-1-63118-480-2)

Audio Versions are also available on Audible, Amazon and Apple

Other Books in this Series and Related Titles

Rosicrucian Rules, Secret Signs, Codes and Symbols by various (978-1-63118-488-8)

History and Teachings of the Rosicrucians by W W Westcott &c (978-1-63118-487-1)

The Mysteries of Freemasonry & the Druids by various (978-1-63118-444-4)

Masonic Symbolism in Shakespeare by Clegg & McDaniel (978-1-63118-472-7)

Ancient Egyptian Mysteries and Hieroglyphics, Modern Freemasonry & Initiation of the Pyramid by Evans, Newton, M P Hall &c (978-1-63118-430-7)

Freemasonry and the Egyptian Mysteries by C. W. Leadbeater (978-1-63118-456-7)

Qabbalistic Teachings and the Tree of Life by M P Hall (978-1-63118-482-6)

Symbolism of the Corner Stone, the North East Corner and the Religious & Masonic Symbolism of Stones by Albert G Mackey &c (978-1-63118-412-3)

Cloud Upon the Sanctuary by K. Eckartshausen (978-1-63118-438-3)

The Eleusinian Mysteries and Rites by Dudley Wright (978–1–63118–530–4)

Royal Arch, Capitular and Cryptic Masonry by Waite &c (978-1-63118-425-3)

The Psalms of Solomon by King Solomon (978-1-63118-439-0)

The Book of Wisdom of Solomon by King Solomon (978-1-63118-502-1)

Masonic Symbolism of Easter and the Christ in Masonry (978-1-63118-434-5)

The Odes of Solomon by King Solomon (978-1-63118-503-8)

Ancient Mysteries and Secret Societies by M P Hall (978-1-63118-410-9)

The Golden Verses of Pythagoras: Five Translations (978-1-63118-479-6)

A Few Masonic Sermons by A. C. Ward &c (978-1-63118-435-2)

The Story and Legend of Hiram Abiff by Albert G Mackey &c (978-1-63118-411-6)

The Legend of the Holy Grail and its Connection with Templars and Freemasons by A E Waite (978-1-63118-462-8)

Audio versions are also available on Audible, Amazon and Apple

Table of Contents

Series Introduction…7

Initiation and the Great Mysteries

Part I…9

Part II…31

INTRODUCTION

The word "esoteric" can be difficult to define. Esotericism in general can be seen less as a system of beliefs and more as a category, which encompasses numerous, different systems of beliefs. It's a bit of juxtaposition, since the word "esoteric" indicates something that few people know about, while the term itself broadly covers numerous philosophies, practices, areas of study and belief systems.

In a greater sense, Esotericism acts as a storehouse for secret knowledge, which is often considered ancient *(by tradition, if not by fact),* passed down from generation to generation, in private. At various times in history, simply possessing the knowledge of some of these subjects, was considered illegal and a jailable offence, if discovered. This usually included such general topics as Alchemy, Pharmacology, Qabalah, Hermeticism, Occultism, Ceremonial Magic, Astrology, Divination, Rosicrucianism and so on. Collectively, these areas of study were often referred to as the esoteric sciences.

Sometimes, the outer garment of a subject isn't esoteric, while what is hidden beneath it, is. As an example, Freemasonry isn't necessarily esoteric by nature (at *least not anymore),* but certain signs, passwords and handshakes given to the candidate during their initiation, are in fact, esoteric, in the sense that they are hidden from the general public.

Today, in the twenty-first century, such topics are readily available at bookstores across the country, and numerous mainsteam publishers offer beginners guides and coffee-table volumes on many of these subjects, intended for mass appeal. Books like *"The Secret"* have turned previously arcane topics into household knowledge. All that being the case, however, it isn't to say that there still aren't buried secrets to uncover, ancient wisdom being ignored and forgotten mysteries to be explored. In fact, it is often that we are only able to further our own studies by standing on the shoulders of these disappearing giants.

Lamp of Trismegistus is doing its part to help preserve humanity's esoteric history by making some of these classics available to those students who are seeking to unearth the knowledge of these ancient colossi.

So, be sure to check other titles from our *Esoteric Classics* series, as well as our *Occult Fiction, Theosophical Classics, Foundations of Freemasonry Series, Supernatural Fiction, Paranormal Research Series, Studies in Buddhism* and our *Christian Apocrypha Series.* You can also download the audio versions of most of these titles from Amazon, Apple or Audible, for learning on the go.

INITIATION AND THE GREAT MYSTERIES

PART I

It is a well-known fact that the biographies of all the great World-Saviors closely resemble each other. All are represented as divinely begotten, and born at the same time of the year; all are threatened with death in infancy; all are tempted, persecuted, and finally slain; all descend into hell and after three days rise from the dead; and at last all ascend into heaven and become glorified Gods.

What is the explanation of this wonderful similarity in the lives of Jesus, Apollonius, Mithra, Buddha, Krishna, Zoroaster, etc.? The solution of this remarkable identity is to be found in the fact that all these Saviors were Initiates into the Mysteries of Antiquity. The various narratives do not describe the physical life of the heroes, but the inner mystic life, being but a materialization of the mystic life of the Initiate. The physical plane biographies might greatly vary, but their lives as Initiates are ever the same.

In our study of the meaning of true Initiation we shall see the origin of these stories. I will commence at the beginning and trace the various stages of progress.

In the first place, a man to be recognized as a candidate, must be pure and holy, and possess a well-developed and well-trained mind. Having attained the exoteric "good life," he enters on the preparation for Initiation. Certain conditions have now to be fulfilled and certain attributes acquired. The aspirant for Initiation must be "worthy and well qualified, duly and truly prepared." During this period the candidate is said to be treading the Probationary Path, the Path which leads up to the "Strait Gate," beyond which is the "Narrow Way," or the "Path of Holiness," the "Way of the Cross," which leadeth unto life.

Let me briefly sum up the attributes to be acquired:

1. Discrimination. This means that the aspirant becomes able to distinguish between the Eternal and the Temporal, the Real and the Unreal, so that what is unreal to. the world becomes real to him. He must set his affections on things above, loosen the ties on worldly objects, and fix his aspirations on things pertaining to the unseen. This has been called "allegiance to the Higher Self."

2. Devotion to Right. The aspirant here learns to do what is right because it is right, without regard to his own gain or loss. This is sometimes called indifference to personal reward as the fruit of good actions. This indifference is the natural result of the previous step, men cease to crave for earthly rewards when they realize their impermanent character.

3. The six qualifications (a) Control of Thoughts—purity and calmness which result from control of the mind, (b) Control of Actions—mastery of one's actions and words. (c) Tolerance—freedom from bigotry, from

an exaggerated attachment to any doctrinal belief, leading to a wide impartiality, (d) Forbearance—freedom from resentment in respect to real or fancied wrongs, (e) Steadfastness—incapability of being turned aside from one's purpose, (f) Faith—confidence in the power of the Master to teach the truth, and of one's self to grasp and wield it.

4. Direct Order or Succession—a clearly defined desire for spiritual existence, and union with the higher ideals.

5. Readiness for Initiation—the result of the previous acquirements.

The candidate is not expected to fully develop these attributes, he must, however, have made progress in them before he is ready for the first step on the Path Proper.

When the time comes that he is regarded fit for Initiation, he is conducted by the Master, who has been watching over his earlier progress, to the threshold where the "Guardians of the Mysteries" open for him the "Strait Gate."

The Path Proper is divided into four stages, or five stages with the culmination. In the first four stages—the period between the good man and the triumphant Master—the neophyte is to cast off the ten fetters that bind him to the circle of rebirth, and which keep him from realizing Nirvana—the highest state of spiritual consciousness. No partial success will here suffice, he must be entirely free before he can pass from one stage to the next. When these fetters are cast off the ego is ready for the fifth stage—full adeptship. lie becomes an "Asekha" Adept—a Christ Triumphant. The first step in the Hindu system is called Sotapatti or Sohan. One who attains this level is called the Sotapanna or Sowani—he who has entered the stream, one who has begun the higher human evolution. This evolution is that of the Divine Child, and is called in different systems by different names—Christ, Horus, Buddha, etc.

It was at this first great Initiation that the Divine Child was born in man. This was spoken of as the "New" or "Second Birth"—a mystic term often employed to denote the rites of Initiation. In India, even to-day, the higher castes are called the "twice born," and the ceremony that makes them such is called Initiation. The rite of baptism is connected with the first Initiation.' It is a symbol of purification, and signifies that the candidate has attained the purity of character necessary for acceptance. "In all these Mysteries," masonic authority Albert Mackey has to say, "the first step taken by the candidate was a lustration or purification. The aspirant was not permitted to enter the sacred vestibule, or take any part in the secret formula of Initiation, until, by water or by fire, he was emblematically purified from the corruptions of the world which he was about to leave behind."[1] The purification of the body was symbolic of a purification of the heart.

Frederic Portal, in speaking of the Egyptian Mysteries, says, "In Egyptian Cosmogony... water was the mother of the

---

[1] *Symbolism of Freemasonry*, Mackey, p. 93.

world, the matrix of all created beings. Man was considered as an image of the world, the Initiate was to be born again to a new life and the baptism thenceforward symbolized the primeval waters; it was on this account that the Initiate was called "Moses," a word signifying in Egyptian, according to Josephus, saved from the water, or by the water... water was a symbol of purity and designated the birth of the pure or Initiated."[2] Again, he says, speaking of the method of Egyptian baptism, "Horus and Thoth-Lunus pour water on the head of the candidate, who is transformed to divine life and to purity." The legend accompanying this scene he translates thus, "Horus, son of Isis, baptises with water and fire." This is repeated three times. The name given to the baptized or anointed, as we have seen, was Moses, signifying regenerated, or begotten again. Remember the lawgiver of the Jews was called by the Egyptians Moses—one saved by water, or, in other words, one Initiated. In the Acts of the Apostles we are told that Moses was learned in all the wisdom of the Egyptians; if so, he must have been an Initiate. The great Mystery of Egypt was this second birth, the Birth of Horus. Says W. Marsham Adams, "Throughout the sacred writings of Egypt, there is no doctrine of which more frequent mention is made than that of a divine birth."[3]

The candidate was initiated from the Sacred Roll, called the "Book of the Greatest Mysteries," and after passing the Passage of the Sun, the crown of Illumination was placed upon his head. And now the new twice-born, "clothed in power and

---
[2] *A Comparison of Egyptian Symbols with those of the Hebrews*, p. 81.
[3] *The Egyptian Doctrine of Light*, Adams, p. 89.

crowned with light, traverses the abodes or scenes of his former weakness, there to discern, by his own enlightened perception, how it is 'Osiris who satisfies the balance of Him who rules the Heavens; to exert in its supernal freedom his creative will, now the Lord, not the slave of the senses; and to rejoice in the just suffering which wrought his Illumination and Mastery."[4]

Hermes in the "Secret Sermon on the Mountain," discourses on the secret of the New Birth. This might well be called the "Initiation of Tat." The sermon is in the form of a dialogue between Hermes the Master and Tat the pupil. Tat says, "In the General Sermons, father [a technical name of the Master or Initiator], thou didst speak in riddles most unclear, conversing on Divinity; and when thou saidst no man could e'er be saved before Rebirth, thy meaning thou didst hide. Further, when I became thy Suppliant, in Wending up the Mount, after thou hadst conversed with me, and when I longed to learn the Sermon (Logos) on Rebirth, (for this beyond all other things is just the thing I know not), thou saidst, that thou wouldst give it me—'when thou shalt have become a stranger to the world.' Wherefore I got me ready and made the thought in me a stranger to the world-illusion."

G. R. S. Mead, in his "Thrice Greatest Hermes," in commenting upon this discourse, says, "The Mne has come for Tat to receive, through his Master, the touch of the true Mind in Consciousness, the Christ is to be born in his heart, the light of the Pleroma is to shine in his inmost being. It is to be a New

---

[4] Ibid, p. 185.

Birth, a Regeneration, or Rebirth, in the sense of being born from Above."⁵

Tat had made himself ready for this Rebirth by passing through three stages of probation. He had been prepared by "Wending up the Mount." The phrase "On the Mountain" or "Wending up the Mountain" is symbolical of the grades of Initiation. The term is of frequent occurence in the Christian Gnostic and Apochryphal writings, and everywhere signifies the "Mount of Initiation." In the popular beliefs, the mountain is called the "Mount of Galilee," on which all the rites of Initiation were performed. But the real "Mount" was no physical elevation, it was the "height of contemplation, an inner state of spiritual consciousness." Tat had been wending his way up this "Mount" and was now ready for the New Birth, "The crowning mystery of the Spiritual Way for all the mystic schools of the time."

"The secret that Tat would learn is the Mystery of the birth from the Virgin Womb—the Birth of Man, the Great Mystery of Regeneration."⁶ Tat entreats Hermes to explain to him the manner of this Rebirth. But Hermes cannot tell to Tat the secret in words. It must be self-perceived. "This race my child," says Hermes, "was never taught." This is the "Race" referred to by Philo as the "Race of Devotees who are ever taught more and more to see, let them strive for the Initiation of That which-is; let them transcend the sun which men perceive [and gaze upon the Light beyond, the True Sun or

---

⁵ *Thrice Greatest Hermes*, Mead, Vol. II, p. 239.
⁶ Ibid, p. 240.

Logos,] nor ever leave this rank which leads to Perfect Blessedness. Now they who betake themselves to the [Divine] Service [do so], not because of any custom or on someone's advice or appeal, but carried away with Heavenly Love, like those Initiated into the Bacchic and the Corybantic Mysteries; they are afire with God until they behold the object of their love." Again Philo says, "Now this natural class of men [lit. race] is to be found in many parts of the inhabited world; for both the Grecian and non-Grecian world must needs share in the perfect Good."[7] This "Race," then, was the Race of Initiates, the "Race of Elxai" mentioned by Epiphanius. Those attaining this state apprehended the mystery of Rebirth.

Although this spiritual state could not be taught to the neophyte in words, still, as Mead puts it, Hermes can guide Tat toward the realization of the Blessed Sight, by putting himself into the sublime state of consciousness, that Tat, so to speak, bathes, or is baptized in his Alaster's spiritual presence—the Cup of the Mind. This is the true laying on of hands. Hermes describes the change that takes place in himself when he passes into the high spiritual consciousness. "Whene'er I see within myself the Simple Vision. . . I have passed through myself into a Body that can never die. And now I am not what I was before; but I am born in Mind." The Master focusses his consciousness in the higher part of his spiritual nature—transfers it to a spiritual vehicle. "The way to do this is not taught, and it cannot be seen by the compound element by means of which thou seest," that is, it cannot be understood from any sensible experience. No physical sight can penetrate this Mystery.

---

[7] Philo on *The Contemplative Life*.

"Thou seest me with eyes, my son," says Hermes, "but what I am thou dost not understand." The outer physical form of the Master was there, but his soul had been liberated from the body.

This mystery could only be understood by one who himself had reached the higher state.

Tat's spiritual senses are being born by the aid of the Master. He says, "Into fierce frenzy and mind fury hast thou plunged me, father, for now no longer do I see myself." He is losing touch with the physical plane consciousness, but that is not enough. Hermes says, "I would, my son, that thou had'st e'en passed right through thyself," that is, passed into the higher vehicle, "the body that can never die." This is the mystery that Hermes could not explain in words.[8]

Isis is not permitted to declare the secret of Rebirth openly to Horus. She says, "I may not tell the story of this birth; for it is not permitted to declare the origin of thy descent, O Horus, son of mighty power, lest afterward the Way-of-Birth of the immortal Gods should be known unto men."[9] the Isis mystery tradition we find that it was a part of the word to bestow this higher consciousness. Diodorus informs us that it was Isis who "discovered the Philtre of immortality, by means of which, when her son Horus, who had been plotted against by the Titans, and found dead beneath the waters, not only raised him to life, but also made him a sharer in immortality."

---

[8] *The Secret Sermon on the Mountain.*
[9] Quoted in *Thrice Greatest Hermes*, Vol. II, p. 242.

Initiation bestowed or restored to the soul the consciousness of immortality. This was truly a new birth, an inner change, a "striking of a new keynote." He who is reborn into the Gnosis, passes from man into the state of super-man. The very essence of Gnosis is the fact that man can transcend his present limitations, and become consciously divine. This is true illumination. Those who attained this Hermes or Horus state were to keep silent concerning their powers, and not boast of their Gnosis.

We find this same teaching in the Christian Mysteries. Jesus says, "Except a man be born again he cannot see the Kingdom of God."[10] Peter says, "Seeing ye have purified your souls in obeying the truth. . . being born again not of corruptible seed but of incorruptible, by the word of God which liveth and abideth forever."[11]

The birth is spoken of as that of "water and the spirit." In the Mysteries of Jesus, as in all others, baptism was always connected with the first Initiatory Rite. Many illustrations of this pivot doctrine of the early church might be cited from Gnostic writings. The overwriter of the Naassene Document tells us that the Lesser Mysteries pertain to fleshly generation, whereas the Greater, deal with the new or second birth, with regeneration and not with genesis. In speaking of the Mystery of Regeneration, the writer says, "For this is the Gate of Heaven, and this is the House of God, where the Good God dwells alone; into which [house] no impure [man] shall come—

---

[10] John, III. 3.
[11] I Peter I. 22, 23.

no psychic, no fleshly [man]— but it is kept under watch for the spiritual alone—where, when they come, they must cast away their garments, and all become bridegrooms, obtaining their true manhood through the Virginal Spirit. For this is the Virgin, big with Child, conceiving and bearing a son—not psychic, not fleshly, but a blessed Aeon of Aeons," that is, an immortal God. This is the birth of the Christ, or Horus in man, the Great Mystery that awaits us when we have made ourselves strangers to the world illusion, as Hermes puts it, or as Jesus says in one of his new found sayings, "Except ye fast to the world, ye shall in no wise find the Kingdom of God." This writing is important, as it shows that the inner teaching of Christianity was identical with the tenets of the other Mysteries—Eleusinian, Egyptian, Mithraic, Dionysian, etc. The date of this Christian over-writer was about the middle of the second century.

In the mystery ritual of Initiation in the "Acts of John," we read, "Who I am, thou shalt know when I depart [that is, by contrast]. What I am seen to be, that am I not; but what I am, thou shalt see when thou comest." In other words, this spiritual state must be realized to be known, and only those who had attained the Christ state—the Perfect Initiate— could know it. Remember the words of Hermes already cited, "Thou seest me with eyes, my son; but what I am thou dost not understand." This consciousness transcends man's normal state.

Although the new birth primarily signified the first great Initiation, when the white robed neophyte entered the "Communion of Saints," still, the mystic term might well indicate the other stages of soul development, for it signalized the entrance to a new life. The Initiate is ushered into a new state of consciousness at each stage, as much so as the new born infant when ushered into physical existence. It is difficult for us to imagine these higher states of consciousness, but each state ushered the candidate into a new realm, where, while retaining hold on the physical plane, he had to adapt himself to new conditions. Each rite was a sign and symbol of spiritual consciousness which had come to the new born disciple. "The Christ principle, the intuitional Wisdom, is born in the soul, and when that Buddhic [spiritual] consciousness is awakened, the soul becomes again, as it were, a little child, born into that higher life of the Initiated, which is in truth the Kingdom of Heaven."[12] The new born Son, the "little child," a technical term denoting one just Initiated, is now to live the divine life and become "like unto the Father"—pass from Sonship to Perfection.

The new or spiritual birth, then, is a mystic fact. The materialization of this inner truth into the dogma of the "Virgin Birth" must have been a comparatively late development in the evolution of popular or general Christianity. The dogma is not to be found in the common document, and the earlier traditions all state that Joseph was the natural father of Jesus. Celsus accused the Christians of changing their gospel story many times in order to better answer the objections of opponents. This is true only of the exoteric tradition.

---

[12] *Christian Creed*, Leadbeater, p. 76.

Now let us consider the various stages in the evolution of the Christ in man. To understand this higher evolution, which constituted the work of the True Mysteries, we must understand man's constitution.

We will use' here the Christian terminology because of familiarity with the terms, but the facts described are the same in all systems.

Christian theology usually accepts the three-fold division—Spirit, Soul and Body. This is sound, but in order to understand the Mystery of the life of the Divine Child, especially his crucifixion, resurrection and ascension, we shall need a further subdivision of man's constitution. The spirit is itself a trinity, containing the three aspects of the divine life—Intelligence, Love and Will; the soul is twofold, composed of the mind and emotional nature; the body is the material instrument of the soul and spirit, and is also dual, being composed of the dense physical body and its etheric double. These lower portions or principles—the dual physical body, the desire or emotional body, and the mental body—form the natural body spoken of by of St. Paul. The Apostle says, "There is a natural body and there is a spiritual body." The spiritual is made up of the three higher principles. The lowest of these is sometimes called the Causal body, the second division the Bliss or Glorified or resurrected body, the third and highest division, the Atmic body.

These principles or bodies are correlated with the lower five of the seven planes of our universe. The normal evolution of mankind takes place on the three lowest planes; the Supernormal evolution, that of the Initiate, proceeds on the next two planes which are the spiritual. These five planes constitute the field of the evolution of consciousness until the "human merges into the divine."

Bearing these divisions of man's constitution in mind and the planes to which they are correlated, we are ready to study the mystery of the Christ evolution. This evolution is set forth in the story of the Mystic Christ. The Mystic Christ is one aspect of the Christ of the Mysteries. The Mystic Christ deals with this Christ evolution, which is the development of the Love, or second aspect, of the unfolding divine spirit in man, called the Christ; the other aspect, called the Mythic Christ, is the Logos, the second Aspect or Person of the Trinity, descending into matter.

The development of the first division of the spiritual body, the aspect of intelligence, takes place in the ordinary life of the world. When this intellectual development has been carried to a high point, accompanied by moral development, then the man is ready for the evolution of the second aspect of the spirit, the second division of the spiritual body, that of Love, called the Christ.

We will consider first this aspect of the Mystic Christ—the evolution of the Christ of the human spirit. This is the "Christ who is in every one of us, who is born and lives, is crucified, rises from the dead, and ascends into heaven in every suffering and triumphant Son of Man." This is the story of the mystic life of every Initiate.

We have seen that at the first great Initiation the Christ is born in the disciple. This is the second birth to which we have referred. He is born into the Kingdom of Heaven as a little child—the name given to a new Initiate. Jesus said that except a man becomes as a little child he cannot enter the Kingdom.

Every such child is beset by perils that do not befall others. The dark powers seek his undoing, but the Christ child once born cannot be destroyed. He grows in wisdom and spiritual stature until the time comes for the second great Initiation, symbolized by the baptism "by water and the spirit," which confers on him the powers necessary for the Teacher. He then goes forth into the world to labor, and is led by the Spirit into the wilderness, and is there exposed to severe temptations. The evil powers strive to lure him from his set purpose, bidding him use his unfolding powers to secure worldly ends. But triumphant over those temptations, he uses the powers which he would not employ for his own needs, to save the world. This devotion to service leads him to the third great Initiation, symbolized by the Transfiguration. He again ascends "the mountain apart," the sacred mount of initiation, but he cannot there remain. He sets his face resolutely toward Jerusalem, where he is to meet the baptism of the Holy Ghost and of Fire—the final test and the last stage of the "Way of the Cross." He is now ready for the fourth great Initiation, symbolized by the passion. He has become victorious over the lower nature, and is willing to nail it to the cross. Although he enters into Jerusalem in triumph and in full confidence that he is prepared for the sacrifice, there comes the bitter agony in the garden, and for a moment he prays that the cup may pass—that bitter cup of betrayal, desertion and pain, when in the horrors and darkness of this final trial it seems that even the Father has forsaken him. His inner vision is blinded, and he thinks himself alone; but he is still steadfast, and with an unconquering trust he yields up the lower life, and descends into hell, that no region in the universe may remain untrodden. But liberated from the material body he sees the light once more, and feels himself again as the Son, and is ready for the fifth Initiation, symbolized by the resurrection and ascension, and rises triumphant over death and hell; then He remains for a time on earth to teach his disciples, and at last ascends into Heaven.

This story of the gospel biography sets forth in allegory the life history of every Initiate. The initiatory rites symbolize the stages through which the candidate passes. The stage of the soul's progress typified by death, burial and resurrection, was called in Egypt "the death rite," and by the Gnostic Christians "the Initiation of the Cross."

The candidate was received by the initiating Hierophant at the proper time and place, usually a secluded chamber in a temple or pyramid, and laid on the stone floor with arms outstretched; sometimes on a wooden cross, which was hollowed out to support the human figure. He was then touched with the thyrsus, the "spear of the crucifixion," on the heart; he then passed into a deep trance. The body was placed in a sarcophagus of stone, a vault or tomb beneath the floor of the Hall of Initiation, and carefully guarded. Meantime, while the body was dead and buried, he himself was fully alive in the invisible world (Hades), and undergoing what was called the tests of earth, water, fire and air. He then put on his perfected Bliss Body, which was now fully organized as a vehicle of consciousness. After the third day the cross, bearing the body, was lifted up and carried out into the air on the east side of the pyramid or temple and placed on a sloping surface ready to greet the rising sun. At the moment the first rays touched the face, the perfected Initiate, the Horus or Christ, rose from the dead, resuscitated the body, and glorified it by his resurrected body, no longer a natural man but a spiritual man, having overcome death and hell.

The trance typifies his "death unto sin"; the revival, his "rebirth or resurrection unto righteousness." In the "Acts of John" there is preserved the tradition of the inner schools on the mystery of the "Initiation of the Cross." We find here no trace of the literal historic tradition. The crucifixion was an inner experience of the soul. The cross was a symbol of the crucifixion of the soul in the matter and its regeneration. "Mystical death," says Dr. Hartman, "is identical with spiritual regeneration."[13] The cross also symbolizes cosmic processes. If the "Acts of John" had given the drama of Initiation, as well as the liturgy, we should undoubtedly have seen that the passion of Christ was something quite different from what has been popularly supposed. I have shown in the preceding lectures that

---

[13] *Magic White and Black*, Hartman, p. 185.

the symbolic rites of "crucifixion" and the "resurrection of the dead," were connected with the most world-wide mystic festivals of antiquity, a highly important fact, for it enables us to understand the meaning of the Christian crucifixion and resurrection.

When the neophyte reached a certain stage of perfection or enlightenment, he was said to "rise from the dead." The phrase "resurrection from the dead" is a mystical phrase used to represent the new birth or resurrection, the Gnostic illumination. When the candidate reached this stage he was immortal — had attained unbroken consciousness of his spiritual ego; he became now the triumphant Christ, "I am he that liveth and was dead; and behold, I am alive for-evermore, Amen; and have the keys of hell' and death."[14]

Let me here cite several authorities regarding this important ceremony: Dr. Oliver, speaking of Initiation, says, "It was considered to be a mystical death or oblivion of all the stains and imperfections of a corrupted and evil life, as well as a descent into hell, where every pollution was purged by lustrations of fire and water; and the perfect Epopt was then said to be regenerated or new born, restored to a renovated existence of life, light and purity, and placed under divine protection."[15] In his "Signs and Symbols," he again says, "In all the Ancient Mysteries, before an aspirant could claim to participate in the higher secrets of the institution, he was placed within the Pastos, or Bed, or Coffin; or, in other words, was

---

[14] Rev. I, 18.
[15] *History of Initiation*, Oliver, p. 11.

subjected to a solitary confinement for a prescribed period of time, that he might reflect seriously, in seclusion and darkness, on what he was about to undertake. This was the symbolical death of the mysteries, and his deliverance from confinement was the act of regeneration or being born again; or, as it was also termed, being raised from the dead. . . The ceremony here alluded to was, doubtless, the same as the descent into Hades. . . His resurrection from the bed [or tomb] was his restoration to life, or his regeneration into a new world; and it was virtually the same as his return from Hades. . . The candidate was made to undergo these changes in scenic representation; and was placed under the Pastos in perfect darkness, generally for the space of three days and nights."[16]

Dr. Mackey says, "The vault was, in the Ancient Mysteries, symbolic of the grave, for Initiation was symbolic of death, where alone divine Truth is to be found."[17] He again says, "The intention of the ceremonies of Initiation into them, was, by a scenic representation of death, and subsequent restoration to life, to impress the great truths of the resurrection of the dead and the immortality of the soul. . . They were all funereal in their character; they began in sorrow and lamentation, they ended in joy; there was an aphanism, or burial; a pastos, or grave; an eure-sis, or discovery of what had been lost; and a legend, or mythical relation—all of which were entirely and profoundly symbolical in their character."[18]

---

[16] *Signs and Symbols*, Oliver, p. 78.
[17] *Encyclopedia of Freemasonry*, Mackey, p. 852.
[18] *The Symbolism of Freemasonry*, Mackey, p.38.

Faber says, "The Initiation into the Mysteries scenically represented the mystic descent into Hades and the return from thence to the light of day."[19]

Many other authorities might be cited in evidence of this ceremony, but this will suffice to prove the ceremony universal and connected with all the Mystery Institutions.

The saying of Jesus that the "Son of Man shall remain three days and three nights in the heart of the earth," corresponds with the ancient rite, but in the gospel story of the resurrection the interval from Friday evening to Sunday morning cannot be regarded as three days and three nights. It has been suggested that the shortening of the time was due to the fact that in the degeneracy of the Mysteries, where attempts were made to minimize all requirements, the original period became so tedious to candidates who could not pass into the trance, that the time was reduced from seventy-two hours to twenty-seven, by just reversing the figures, thus saving the candidate nearly two full days of solitary confinement. The materialized gospel story, evidently followed this later practice.

These great rites stood originally for great spiritual truths. The body with which the candidate "rose from the dead" was the Bliss Body—the body of the Christ which had been developed during the period of service on earth. This body belongs to the life of the Initiate—the Christ life. Its building begins at the second birth, when the Christ is born in man, and reaches its completion at the resurrection. During this

---

[19] *Origin of Pagan Idolatry*, Faber, Vol. IV., p. 34.

evolutionary period, when the Son is "being made perfect" the Initiate is called the "Son of Man;" the perfected, risen, and glorified Christ is called the "Son of God."

There is still another feature of the Christ story— the Ascension. This has to do with the third part of the spiritual body, the putting on of the Atmic body, or the Vesture or Robe of Glory, as it is called n the Pistis Sophia. Spiritual evolution consists in the organization and vitalization of the various Garments or Sheaths of man into Vestures or Robes of Power and Glory, for the use of the Regenerate in the "Path of Ascent," the "Way Above." The highest Vesture prepares the Son for union with the Father, and as a spiritual fact this is symbolized by the Ascension. The material story of the Ascension is an historicization of this inner mystic truth, experienced by every soul that becomes consciously one with God.

"The ascension for humanity is when the whole race has attained the Christ condition, the state of the Son, and that Son becomes one with the Father, and God is all in all. That is the goal, prefigured in the triumph of the Initiate, but reached only when the human race is perfected and when 'the great orphan, Humanity,' is no longer an orphan, but consciously recognizes itself as the Son of God."[20]

---

[20] *Esoteric Christianity*, Besant, p. 249.

PART II

We have seen in the preceding lecture that the Christ of the Mysteries has two aspects— the Mystic and the Mythic. In the Mystic, the Microcosm, Man, the Christ of the Mysteries, represents the second aspect of the divine spirit in humanity, called the Christ; in the Mythic, the Macrocosm, the Cosmos, the Christ of the Mysteries, represents the Logos in His manifestation through His Second Aspect.

In the preceding lecture we have studied the Mystic Christ; now we are to consider the Mythic Christ.

The great facts of the spiritual life were carefully guarded in the Mysteries, and given out to the world only in symbolic language. The Solar or Sun-Myth is the popular teaching concerning the Cosmic Mythic Christ—the Christ of the Solar Myths or legends. A Myth we must remember is not mere fiction; it may be truer than written history; it is a great truth embodied in a pictorial form. All symbols were employed by Initiates with a definite meaning; we need, therefore, to know the true meaning of the symbols in order to read the true meaning of the Myth.

The Solar-Myth sets forth, primarily, the activity of the Logos (the Mythic Christ) in the universe; secondarily, the mystic life of the In date. This story of the Sun-God, then, is of utmost importance. It begins with his birth at the winter solstice, after the shortest day of the year, in the early morning hours of Dec. 25th, as the sign Virgo is rising above the horizon. He is thus born of a Virgin who remains such after giving birth to her Sun-Child, for the celestial Virgo is still unchanged. In the ancient drawings Virgo of the Zodiac is represented as a woman suckling a child; here we find the origin of the symbol of the Madonna.

The Sun-God is weak and feeble in his infancy— born at the period when the days are shortest and the nights longest, as with us on this side of the equatorial line. He is beset by perils in his early youth, but he outlives the threatening dangers of darkness and storm, and grows to manhood. However, he is rapidly approaching his crucifixion, and the glorious days preceding the spring equinox are soon to be clouded by the solar disturbances incident upon his crossing the line. This crossing was called the crucifixion, the date varying with each year. But like all so-called death it is an illusion— merely a transition to a higher life. The Sun-God soon rises triumphantly and ascends into heaven—the storms are dissipated and darkness gives way to all-conquering light. Jupiter, Osiris, Ormuzd, Apollo, are victorious over all their foes. All nature rejoices, celebrating their conquest, and order is re-established in place of the dire confusion that reigned while gloomy Typhon or Ahriman was dominant. Thus everywhere we find the fable that typifies the triumph of Light over darkness. The Sun could not be kept entombed by the elements. He rose from the dead and ascended into heaven, where, at the Summer Solstice, he attained the acme of his glory and perfection. There he rules triumphant and gives his very life to ripen the fruit and grain and so sustain his worshipers.

These are the salient points in the lives of all the Sun-Gods, for each is born on the 25th of December, and crucified at the Vernal equinox. The birth-date is fixed, while the death-date is variable. This of itself should be sufficient to show us that both Christmas and Easter (the Sunday following the next full moon after the vernal equinox) were originally solar festivals. A festival calculated by the relative positions of sun and moon, was not designed to commemorate the anniversary of any historical event. We are not here dealing with the history of a man, but with the Hero of a solar myth.

It is interesting to note that the fast preceding the Easter festival is world-wide, and in many countries extended to the time limit of our modern Lent— forty days. Of course, the original period was only the time intervening between the death and resurrection.

Another interesting fact in this connection is that the animal adopted as the symbol of the Hero is the sign of the Zodiac in which the Sun is at the vernal equinox of his age, and this varies with the precession of the equinoxes. Thus Oannes and Jesus had the sign Pisces—the Fishes; Mithra and Osiris Taurus—the Bull; Jupiter-Ammoir Aries—the Lamb, etc., while Jesus is also represented as the Lamb.

The Sun-Myth, then, primarily sets forth the activity of the Logos in the Cosmos. This activity is reflected in a partial way in the yearly course of the Sun. The Logos, in His Second Aspect, as the Cosmic-Mythic Christ, descends into matter— becomes incarnate, clothed in "flesh." He thus sacrifices himself by putting on the limitations of matter, entering the womb of matter which is yet virgin, unproductive. This matter has been vivified by the Holy Spirit that it might presently take form and is thus prepared to receive the life of the Second Logos, the Son aspect of God, who took this matter as a vehicle for his energies. The original of the Nicene Creed ran thus, "And was incarnate of the Holy Ghost and the Virgin Mary"—not of the virgin-matter alone, but of matter already pulsating with the life of the Third Logos, so that both the life and the matter surrounded Him as a vesture.

Thus was the descent of the Logos into matter described, in the historicized life of the Saviors, as the "Virgin Birth," and in the Solar Myth as the birth of the Sun-God. The misapprehension of this allegorical illustration, as the life history of a physical human being, and its identification with Jesus, and the various other World-Saviors, was most unfortunate and misleading.

After the incarnation "come the early workings of the Logos in matter, aptly typified by the infancy of the Myth. To all the feebleness of infancy His Majestic powers bow themselves, letting but little play forth on the tender forms they ensoul. Matter imprisons, seems as though threatening to slay, its infant King, whose glory is veiled by the limitations He has assumed. Slowly He shapes it towards high ends, and lifts it into manhood, and then stretches Himself on the cross of matter that He may pour forth from that cross all the powers of His surrendered life... Dead He seems and buried out of sight, but He rises again clothed in the very matter in which He seemed to perish, and carries up His body of now radiant matter into heaven, where it receives the downpouring life of the Father, and becomes the vehicle of man's immortal life. For it is the life of the Logos which forms the garment of the soul in man, and He gives it that men may live through the ages and grow to the measure of his own statue. Truly are we clothed in Him, first materially and then spiritually."[21]

The Logos thus leaves the plane of Infinitude, where He is one with the Father, and becomes incarnate, and is finally crucified in space. This is the crucifixion of Christ, the great cosmic sacrifice, represented by the symbol of the crucified Man, which at last becomes materialized into an actual death by crucifixion. The story thus historicized became attached to the various World-Saviors. But the original crucifixion was not disgrace, for the symbol used to represent this mystery is that of the Heavenly Man, with arms outstretched, pouring life and light into His creatures. The Solar-Myth outlines these great spiritual facts regarding the working of God in the universe.

Every symbol has both a primary and a secondary meaning. The Sun is a symbol of the Logos in its primary meaning, but it also represents anyone who is representative of the Logos. Thus a Great Initiate, sent on a special mission to the world, would, by virtue of his office and mission, have the Sun as his symbol. All who are thus signified would have certain characteristics in common and pass through certain activities, and thus of necessity there would arise similarities in the lives

---

[21] *Esoteric Christianity*, p. 181.

of these ambassadors— their life history as Initiates being outlined by the course of the Sun.

When one becomes an Initiate, or when an Initiate is sent out into the world as a Teacher of men, and especially when a spirit such as Jesus becomes a Hierophant in the Mysteries, then the legends of the Mythic Christ, which have been told of other Great Ones, surround Him and He becomes clothed in the drapery of the Solar-Myth. This is perfectly natural and proper, for the Solar-Myth typifies the various stages of progress through which He has passed, and this symbolism could only be applied to one who had attained- the Christ stage of evolution. With such a one the festival of his nativity became the date when the Son was born in the Virgin, and the sign of the zodiac at the vernal equinox became that of his crucifixion. Although these dates were purely arbitrary, adopted from the Sun-Myth, the facts symbolized by the birth, death, and resurrection were living realities in the Mystic life of every Son of God. The adoption of these dates into the materialized life-story of the Great Saviors is thus readily explained— they were derived from the solar symbolism. The fact that the rites of Initiation and the Solar-Myth both symbolize the same thing, the former primarily typifying the growth of the soul, secondarily the work of the Logos, and vice versa, made the inter-weaving of the symbolism in this particular perfectly natural, especially so as the great solar festivals, the solstices and equinoxes, were the times when the Mysteries were celebrated and the rites of Initiation administered. Thus both the Mythic and Mystic Christ have contributed to the gospel story.

These Sun-Myth stories have recurred through all the ages, having been told and retold in turn of each great Teacher,—the legends of the Mythic Christ, Buddha, Krishna,— mingling with the history of each, and crystallizing about each as an historical personage. But these materialized stories pertain especially to the life of the Son of Man, a distinctive title, not of an individual but an office. When one attains this level and stands in this relation to humanity, then, as a representative of God, the story of the Logos in the Sun becomes his own indeed, for the facts underlying this story have been wholly realized in his spiritual life.

Here we learn the manner in which arose the story of the death, burial and resurrection of a crucified Savior. On the lines of the Solar-Myth and the Initiatory rites, the materializing tendency of man wrought out for itself, in each religion, an historical narrative of a personal Savior, who is virgin born, is crucified, rises from the dead, and finally ascends into heaven; or, the historicizing, may, in some instances, have been purposely done by those who knew,—the popular narrative being written for the multitude in such a way as to set forth the Mysteries allegorically. In either case,—and perhaps both methods played a part (we have abundant proof of the former and many indications of the latter),—the account symbolizes the inner doctrine and sets forth figuratively the occult teaching of the Gnosis. But the real meaning of the symbolical teaching of the Myth and Ritual has been practically lost sight of; most people to-day regard the narratives as the physical life history of individuals. However, there are some who are beginning to understand that the symbolical teaching of the death, burial, and resurrection are but typical of the soul's progress.

Jesus of Nazareth, like Buddha, Krishna, and many others, was draped with the stories of the Logos, and the salient events in the Sun-Myth become the salient events in his physical life. The symbols, once materialized, were attached to each Divine Teacher in turn, giving rise to the wonderful similarities in their respective biographies.

But let us not lose sight of the fact that the mystic birth, baptism, transfiguration, death, resurrection and ascension were realities in the life history of every Initiate. This drama is repeated in every soul that becomes a Christ.

The story of the gospel was originally a religious romance intended for spiritual instruction, but the later bishops of the outer churches, not having the key to the inner meaning, accepted the romance as actual history. It is said that "The 'common document' [which formed the basis of the canonical gospels] is to be traced to the sketch of an ideal life which was intended for purposes of propaganda, and which could be further explained to those who were ready for more definite instructions in the true nature of the Christ-Mystery. To a certain extent it was based on some of the traditions of the actual historic doings of Jesus, but the historical details were often transformed by the light of the mystery-teaching, and much was added in changed form concerning the drama of the Christ Mystery; allegories and parables and actual mystery doings were woven into it, with what appears now to be a consummate art which has baffled for ages the intellect of the world, but which at the time was regarded by the writer as a modest effort at simplifying the spiritual truths of the Inner life, by putting them forward in the form of what we should now call a 'historical romance,' but which in his day was one of the natural methods of haggada and apocalyptic."[22]

The author of this romance never dreamed that the story would be taken otherwise than as he intended it—a symbol, but in the compilation of the canonical accounts much legend and historicized dogma was built around this original romance.

The mystic teaching in this way became accepted first as history and finally as dogma. Irenaeus was one of the chief developers of the dogmas. The Gnostics contended that he and those like him who accepted the crude literal view, did not know the origin and meaning of these things. Papius and Marcion, who were earlier than Irenaeus, insisted that such scripture was not reliable as absolute history. The Gnostics knew how these scriptures were made and they possessed a "memory of the manner of things done and said from the earliest times, and looked with amazement on the narrow and cramping beliefs that the bishops of the outer churches were imposing on Christendom as the only truths of the Christ-revelation. . . This contention of the Gnostics, as of men earlier than Justin and Irenaeus, is still subjudice before the bar of history. It means a total reconstruction of the history of the origins."[23]

---

[22] *Did Jesus Live 100 Years B.C.*, Mead, p. 422.
[23] G.R.S. Mead in *Theosophical Review*, March, '06.

The Gnostics treated the gospel legends, not as history, but as symbolic of cosmic processes and the drama of Initiation. I have already shown that the Gnostics did not accept the crucifixion and resurrection of Jesus as historic facts. Justin Martyr also gives evidence that the early church did not understand these things in a literal sense. He says, "And when we say that the Word (Logos) which is the first begetting of God was begotten without intercourse,—Jesus Christ, our Master,—and that he was crucified, and was dead, and rose again and ascended into heaven, we bring forward no new thing beyond those among you who are called Sons of Zeus. For ye know how many sons the writers who are held in honor among you ascribe to Zeus:— Hermes, the Word (Logos), who was the interpreter and teacher of all; and Asclepius, who was also a healer and was smitten by the bolt [of his sire] and ascended into heaven... [and many others]."[24] Justin Martyr here asserts that the Christians bring forward no new thing in the doctrines of Christ's death, resurrection, and ascension "beyond those among you who are called the 'Sons of Zeus.'" The doctrine, then, was a part of the Mysteries, well known by all who had attained to the state of Sons of God. This mystery could not be understood by the uninitiated, and so Justin appeals to the Sons of Zeus, and assures them that he has no new doctrine.

This is conclusive evidence that at the time of Justin Martyr, 140 to 160 A. D., these great spiritual realities in the Mystic life were not regarded by some, at least, as historical facts.

---

[24] Quoted in *Thrice Greatest Hermes*, Mead, Vol. III, p. 217.

Justin further says, "But as to the Son of God called Jesus,—even though he were only a man [born] in the common way, [yet] because of [his] wisdom is he worthy to be called Son of God; for all writers call God 'Father of men and gods.' And if we say [further] that he was also in a special way, beyond the common birth, begotten of God [as] Word (Logos) of God, let us have this in common with you who call Hermes the Word [Logos] who brings tidings from God."[25]

The Sonship of Jesus, then, was considered the same as that of Hermes. And note also that "begotten of God" did not refer to physical birth, but to something beyond. Justin distinctly stated that Jesus was a man born in the common way. This higher birth by which man was begotten of God, and so became a "Son," was not exceptional with Christianity. In fact, Justin Martyr wants it distinctly understood that he teaches nothing new, but merely claims for Jesus the distinctive title of a Son of God, in the same sense as were Hermes, Asclepius, Dionysus, and others, Sons of God, that is, he claimed Jesus was an Initiate.

Origen also is in accord with Justin Martyr. He speaks of the "mystery of the resurrection" and contrasts this inner doctrine, (which he says is not understood by unbelievers,) with the exoteric doctrine of the resurrection which was known to all and was an article of faith among many.[26] It is quite evident that there was a wide difference between the mystic doctrine of the crucifixion and resurrection, and the popular exoteric faith.

---

[25] Ibid, p. 217.
[26] *Contra Celsum*, Origen, Book I, Ch. VII.

Thus studying the inner teaching of the Mysteries we see that Christ is not a unique personage, but the first fruits—the promise of man-made perfect. The Initiate has ever been thus regarded, for to attain the Christ-state is salvation. "The stage of discipleship was to pass into that of Sonship. The life of the Son was to be lived among men till it was closed by the resurrection, and the glorified Christ became one of the perfected Saviors of the World."[27]

Every man is a potential Christ, and the purpose of evolution is to raise every human being to the sublime degree of a Master Christ.

---

[27] *Esoteric Christianity*, Besant, p. 250.

www.ingramcontent.com/pod-product-compliance
Lightning Source LLC
LaVergne TN
LVHW041502070426
835507LV00009B/759